Lord's Prayer

Other Crossway books by J. I. Packer

Faithfulness and Holiness: The Witness of J. C. Ryle

God's Plans for You

Growing in Christ

Life in the Spirit

*A Passion for Faithfulness:
Wisdom from the Book of Nehemiah*

*A Quest for Godliness:
The Puritan Vision of the Christian Life*

J. I. PACKER

Praying the

Lord's Prayer

:: CROSSWAY®

WHEATON, ILLINOIS

Praying the Lord's Prayer

Copyright © 2007 by J. I. Packer

This book was formerly part of *Growing in Christ*, copyright © 1994 by J. I. Packer, originally published under the title *I Want to Be a Christian*.

Published by Crossway
   1300 Crescent Street
   Wheaton, Illinois 60187

Cover design: The DesignWorks Group, www.thedesignworksgroup.com

First printing, 2007

Printed in the United States of America

Unless otherwise indicated, Scripture quotations are taken from the ESV® Bible (The Holy Bible: English Standard Version®). Copyright © 2001 by Crossway. Used by permission. All rights reserved.

Scripture quotations indicated as from JB are taken from *The Jerusalem Bible*, copyright © 1966, 1967, 1968 by Darton, Longman & Todd Ltd. Used by permission.

Scripture quotations indicated as from NEB are taken from *The New English Bible*, copyright © 1961, 1970 by The Delegates of the Oxford University Press and The Syndics of the Cambridge University Press. Used by permission.

Scripture quotations indicated as from *Phillips* are taken from *The New Testament in Modern English*, copyright © 1958, 1959, 1960, 1972 by J. B. Phillips. Used by permission.

ISBN-13: 978-1-58134-963-4
ISBN-10: 1-58134-963-7
ePub ISBN: 978-1-4335-1773-0
PDF ISBN: 978-1-4335-0694-9
Mobipocket ISBN: 978-1-4335-0849-3

Library of Congress Cataloging-in-Publication Data
Packer, J. I. (James Innell)
   Praying the Lord's prayer / J. I. Packer.
      p. cm.
   "This book was formerly part of Growing in Christ by J. I. Packer,
originally published under the title I want to be a Christian"—
T. p. verso.
   ISBN 13: 978-1-58134-963-4 (hc)
   ISBN 10: 1-58134-963-7
   1. Lord's prayer—Devotional literature. I. Title.
BV230.P23   2007
226.9'606—dc22   2007008246

Crossway is a publishing ministry of Good News Publishers.

V P		25	24	23	22	21	20	19	18
19	18	17	16	15	14	13	12	11	10

To
JIM, TOM,
AND ELISABETH

*who by what they
are even more than
by what they say
share the strength they
have been given*

Contents

The Lord's Prayer

"Pray then like this:
'Our Father in heaven,
hallowed be your name.
Your kingdom come,
your will be done,
on earth as it is in heaven.
Give us this day our daily bread,
and forgive us our debts,
as we also have forgiven our debtors.
And lead us not into temptation,
but deliver us from evil.
[For yours is the kingdom and the power
and the glory, forever. Amen.'"]

MATTHEW 6 : 9 - 1 3

(Material in brackets is found in some ancient manuscripts, though not all.)

Cow creations

Use your stickers to create your story

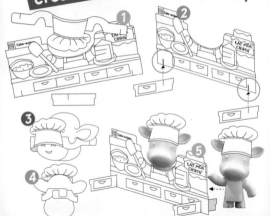

COW creations

creations

Create your cow story

EAT MOR CHIKIN®
Chick-fil-A®

Three venerable formulae together add up to Christianity: the Apostles' Creed, the Ten Commandments, and the Lord's Prayer, summarizing respectively the Christian way of believing, behaving, and communing with God.

The Lord's Prayer in particular is a marvel of compression, and full of meaning. It is a compendium of the gospel (Tertullian), a body of divinity (Thomas Watson), a rule of purpose as well as of petition, and thus a key to the whole business of living. What it means to be a Christian is nowhere clearer than here.

Like other Reformation catechisms, the Anglican Prayer Book Catechism centers on the three summaries. On the Lord's Prayer it says:

> *Question*: What desirest thou of God in this prayer?
>
> *Answer*: I desire my Lord God our heavenly Father, who is the giver of all goodness, to send his grace unto me, and to all people, that we may worship him, serve him, and obey him, as we ought to do. And I pray unto God, that he will send us all things that be needful both for our souls and bodies; and that he will be merciful unto us, and forgive us our sins; and that it will please him to save and defend us in all dangers ghostly [i.e., spiritual] and bodily; and that he will keep us from all sin and wickedness, and from our ghostly enemy, and from everlasting death. And this I trust he will do of his mercy and goodness, through our Lord Jesus Christ. And therefore I say, Amen. So be it.

What these words give us a glimpse of, the following studies will try to spell out.

"Lord, teach us to pray."

LUKE 11:1

CHAPTER 1

When You Pray

Praying to God is a problem for many today. Some go through the motions with no idea why; some have exchanged prayer for quiet thought or transcendental meditation; most, perhaps, have given prayer up entirely. Why the problem? The answer is clear. People feel a problem about prayer because of the muddle they are in about God. If you are uncertain whether God exists, or whether he is personal, or good, or in control of things, or concerned about ordinary folk like you and me, you are bound to conclude that praying is pretty pointless, not to say trivial, and then you won't do it.

But if you believe, as Christians do, that Jesus is the image of God—in other words, that God is Jesus-like in character—then you will have no such doubts, and you will recognize that for us to speak to the Father and the Son in prayer is as

13

natural as it was for Jesus to talk to his Father in heaven, or for the disciples to talk to their Master during the days of his earthly ministry.

TWO-WAY CONVERSATION

Conversations with parents or wise friends whom we love and respect, and who are ready to help us by advice and action, feel neither pointless nor tedious, and we gladly give time to them—indeed, schedule time for them—because we value them, and gain from them. This is how we should think of times of communion with God in prayer. When the Methodist saint Billy Bray said, as he often did, "I must talk to Father about that," it was of praying that he spoke.

Does God, then, really tell us things when we pray? Yes. We shall probably not hear voices, nor feel sudden strong impressions of a message coming through (and we shall be wise to suspect such experiences should they come our way); but as we analyze and verbalize our problems before God's throne, and tell him what we want and why we want it, and think our way through passages and principles of God's written Word bearing on the matter in hand, we shall find many certainties crystallizing in our hearts as to God's view of us and our prayers, and his will for us and others. If you ask, "Why is this or that happening?" no light may come, for "the secret things belong to the LORD our God" (Deuteronomy 29:29); but if you ask, "How am I to serve and glorify God here and now, where I am?" there will always be an answer.

MADE TO PRAY

It is not too much to say that God made us to pray, that prayer is (not the easiest, but) the most *natural* activity in which we ever engage, and that prayer is the measure of us all in God's sight. "What a man is alone on his knees before God," said the saintly Murray McCheyne, "that he is—and no more."

Perhaps Jesus' disciples felt this when they made their momentous request (have you ever echoed it?), "Lord, teach us to pray" (Luke 11:1). Jesus must have rejoiced to be asked this. In the manner of a good teacher, however, he controlled his feelings and gave a matter-of-fact answer. "When you pray, say . . ."—and for the second time in his public ministry he gave them the form of words that we call the Lord's Prayer (Luke 11:2-4; cf. Matthew 6:9-13).

*Prayer is the most **natural** activity in which we ever engage, and prayer is the measure of us all in God's sight.*

"Say . . ." Did Jesus just intend that they should repeat the words, parrot fashion? No; but that they should enter into the sense. "Say," we might say, means "mean!" This prayer is a pattern for all Christian praying. Jesus is teaching that prayer will be acceptable when, and only when, the attitudes, thoughts, and desires expressed fit the pattern. That is to say: every prayer of ours should be a praying of the Lord's Prayer in some shape or form.

LEARNING TO PRAY

"Experience can't be taught!" The phrase comes from a brochure on youth employment, but it is as deep a truth about prayer as it is about wage-earning skills. Praying, like singing, is something you learn to do, not by reading books (not even this one!), but by actually doing it; and it is so natural and spontaneous an activity that you can become quite proficient in it without ever reading up on it. Yet, as voice training helps you to sing better, so others' experience and advice can help us pray to better purpose. The Bible is full of models for prayer: 150 patterns of praise, petition, and devotion are contained in the Psalter, and many more examples of proper praying are recorded too, along with much teaching on the subject.

We should certainly not content ourselves with parroting other people's prayers, nor would God be content if we did (for what parent could be happy if his child only ever spoke to him in quotations, thus limiting his conversation to the reciting of other people's sentiments?). But as another pianist's interpretation of a piece can help a budding musician to see how he can best play it (not, perhaps, in quite the same way), so we are helped to find our own way in prayer by seeing how others have prayed, and indeed by praying with them. And overarching everything we have the Lord's Prayer as our guide.

As analysis of light requires reference to the seven colors of the spectrum that make it up, so analysis of the Lord's Prayer requires reference to a spectrum of seven distinct activities: *approaching* God in adoration and trust; *acknowledging* his work and his worth, in praise and worship; *admitting* sin, and seeking pardon; *asking* that needs be met, for ourselves and others; *arguing* with God for blessing, as wrestling Jacob did in Genesis 32 (God loves to be argued with); *accepting* from God one's own situation as he has shaped it; and *adhering* to God in faithfulness through thick and thin. These seven activities together constitute biblical prayer, and the Lord's Prayer embodies them all.

So the Lord's Prayer should be put to service to direct and spur on our praying constantly. To pray in terms of it is the sure way to keep our prayers within God's will; to pray through it, expanding the clauses as you go along, is the sure way to prime the pump when prayer dries up and you find yourself stuck. We never get beyond this prayer; not only is it the Lord's first lesson in praying, it is all the other lessons too. *Lord, teach us to pray.*

FURTHER BIBLE STUDY

The naturalness of prayer:
• Psalms 27; 139

QUESTIONS FOR THOUGHT AND DISCUSSION

• How does one's view of God affect one's view of prayer?
• Why is prayer "the most natural activity in which we ever engage"?
• In what sense should every prayer be a mirror of the Lord's Prayer?

"Lord, teach us to pray."

LUKE 11:1

CHAPTER 2

Pray Then Like This

"Pray then like this." Thus Jesus introduced the Lord's Prayer in the Sermon on the Mount (Matthew 6:9-13). Clearly, then, the prayer is given to us to be a pattern for our thoughts in prayer as well as a set verbal form. What does the pattern contain? Here is a bird's-eye view.

The address to God (invocation) with which the prayer opens is full of meaning. It must have startled the disciples, for in Judaism calling God "Father" was something one did not do. Jesus directs us, however, to do it—in other words, to seek access and welcome to God's presence on the ground that we are children in his family and he looks on us with a father's love. Then with this we are to link the thought that our Father is "in heaven"—in other words, that he is God, sovereign and self-existent, the God who is both *there* and *in charge*. Fatherly love on the one hand and transcendent greatness on the other are two qualities in God that the rest of the prayer assumes at every point.

Then come three God-centered petitions, voicing together the attitude required by what Jesus called "the great and first commandment—you shall love the Lord your God with all your heart . . ." (Matthew 22:38, 37).

The first petition is that God's "*name*" should be "hallowed." *Name* in the Bible means "person," and the hallowing of God's name means the acknowledging of God as holy through reverence for all his revelation and responsive worship and obedience.

The second petition is that God's "*kingdom*" should come. God's "kingdom" means the public display of his ruling power in salvation, and the prayer for his kingdom to come is a plea that his lordship might be seen and submitted to, and his saving grace experienced, all the world over, till Christ returns and all things are made new.

The third petition asks that God's "*will*" may be done— that is, that all his commands and purposes may be perfectly fulfilled.

GOD FIRST, THEN MAN

Three man-centered petitions follow. By putting them after requests for the exalting of God, the prayer reminds us that we are to ask for the meeting of our particular personal needs *as a means to our Father's glory*, and not in any spirit of trying to bend God's will to our own. We are told to ask for provision of bread, pardon of sins, and protection from temptation and the tempter ("evil" means "the evil one"). All our needs are in principle covered here—all need for material things; all need for spiritual renewing and restoring; all need for guidance and help.

The prayer reminds us that we are to ask for the meeting of our particular personal needs **as a means to our Father's glory,** *and not in any spirit of trying to bend God's will to our own.*

The "praise ending" ascribes to God the "*kingdom*" (that is, it hails him as God on the throne), the "*power*" (that is, it adores him as the God able to do all that we ask), and the "*glory*" (that is, it declares, "we praise thee, O God" here and now). Though early, the manuscripts make it clear that this is not from Christ's own lips—but there is no denying that it fits!

GOD LEADS THE CONVERSATION

When we talk to parents and friends about our anxieties and problems, looking to them for help, they often have to take over leadership in the conversation in order to give it a meaningful shape that our own higgledy-piggledy minds have denied it. We all know what it is to have been pouring out our troubles in full flood and to be pulled up by "Wait a minute; let's get this straight. Now tell me again about so-and-so. . . . Now tell me how you felt about it. . . . Then what's the problem?" Thus they sort us out.

We need to see that the Lord's Prayer is offering us model answers to the series of questions God puts to us to shape our conversation with him. Thus: "Who do you take me for, and what am I to you?" (*Our Father in heaven*.) "That being so, what is it that you really want most?" (*The hallowing of your name; the coming of your kingdom; to see your will known and done*.) "So what are you asking for right now, as a means to that end?" (*Provision, pardon, protection*.) Then the "praise ending" answers the question, "How can you be so bold and confident in asking for these things?" (*Because we know you can do it, and when you do it, it will bring you glory!*) Spiritually, this set of questions sorts us out in a most salutary way.

Sometimes when we pray we feel there is nobody there to listen and are tempted to think that our feelings tell us the truth. What finally dispels this temptation, under God, is a fresh realization (Spirit-given, for sure) that God is actually questioning us in the way described, requiring us to tell him honestly how we think of him and what we want from him and why.

That this is so is part of the teaching of the Lord's Prayer, which from this standpoint is like a child's picture containing a hidden object. At first you look and don't see the object; then it hits you, and every time you look at the picture after that it seems to jump out at you. The hidden object in this case is the God who asks the questions to which the Lord's Prayer, clause by clause, is the proper set of answers. And it is only when you see this that you can use the pattern prayer in the way that its Author and Teacher intended.

FURTHER BIBLE STUDY

A model prayer:
• John 17

QUESTIONS FOR THOUGHT AND DISCUSSION

• On what basis should we seek access to God's presence? Do you think you have such access yourself? What are your reasons for saying yes or no?
• What does the Lord's Prayer have to do with loving God with all our heart?
• Illustrate ways in which the Lord's Prayer might be needed to reshape prayers that we might make.

"If you then, who are evil, know how to give good gifts to your children, how much more will your Father who is in heaven give good things to those who ask him!"

MATTHEW 7 : 11

CHAPTER 3

Our Father

The Lord's Prayer is in family terms: Jesus teaches us to invoke God as our Father, just as he himself did—witness his Gethsemane prayer, for instance, or his High Priestly prayer in John 17, where "Father" comes six times. A question, however, arises. Jesus was God's Son by nature, the second person of the eternal Godhead. We, by contrast, are God's creatures. By what right, then, may we call God *Father*? When Jesus taught this manner of address, was he implying that creaturehood, as such, involves sonship—or what?

ADOPTED

Clarity here is vital. Jesus' point is not that all men are God's children by nature, but that his committed disciples have been adopted into God's family by grace. "To all who received him, who believed in his name, he gave the right to become children of God" (John 1:12). Paul states this as the purpose of the incarnation: "God sent forth his Son . . . so that we might receive adoption as sons" (Galatians 4:4, 5). Prayer to God as Father is for Christians only.

This resolves a puzzle. Elsewhere Jesus stressed that his disciples should pray in his name and through him—that is, looking to him as our way of access to the Father (see John 14:6, 13; 15:16; 16:23-26). Why is there none of this in the model prayer? In fact, the point is present here; it is implicit in "Father." Only those who look to Jesus as Mediator and sin-bearer, and go to God through him, have any right to call on God as his sons.

SONS AND HEIRS

If we are to pray and live as we should, we must grasp the implications of God's gracious fatherhood.

First, as God's adopted children we are *loved* no less than is the one whom God called his "beloved Son" (Matthew 3:17; 17:5). In some families containing natural and adopted children the former are favored above the latter, but no such defect mars the fatherhood of God.

As God's adopted children we are loved no less than is the one whom God called his "beloved Son."

This is the best news anyone has ever heard. It means that, as Paul triumphantly declares, "nothing . . . in all creation, will be able to separate us from the love of God in Christ Jesus our Lord" (Romans 8:39). It means that God will never forget us, or cease to care for us, and that he remains our forbearing Father even when we act the prodigal (as, alas, we all sometimes do).

It means too that, as the Prayer Book says, he is "always more ready to hear than we to pray," and is "wont to give more than either we desire or deserve." "If you then, who are evil," said our Lord, "know how to give good gifts to your children, how much more will your Father who is in heaven give good things to those who ask him!" (Matthew 7:11; the parallel saying in Luke 11:13 has "Holy Spirit" for "good things," and the sustained ministry of the Holy Spirit was surely one of the good things Jesus had in mind). To know this truth of God's fatherly love to us gives boundless confidence not merely for praying, but for all our living.

Second, we are God's *heirs*. Adoption in the ancient world was for securing an heir, and Christians are joint heirs with Christ of God's glory (Romans 8:17). "We are God's children now . . . when he appears we shall be like him" (1 John 3:2). Already "all [things] are yours" in the sense that they further your good here and your glory hereafter, for "you are Christ's" (1 Corinthians 3:21-23; Romans 8:28-30). To grasp this is to know oneself rich and privileged beyond any monarch or millionaire.

Third, we have *God's Spirit* in us. With our changed relationship to God (adoption) goes a change of direction and desire, of outlook and attitude, which Scripture calls regeneration or new birth. Those who "believed in" Jesus' "name" were "born . . . of God" (John 1:12ff.), or more precisely "born of the Spirit" (3:6; see verses 3-8). "Because you are sons," says Paul, "God has sent the Spirit of his Son into our hearts, crying [that is, prompting us to cry, spontaneously, as the expression of a new spiritual instinct], 'Abba! Father!'" (Galatians 4:6). And when, to our distress (and this comes to us all), we find ourselves so muddle-headed, dead-hearted, and tongue-tied in prayer that "we do not know how to pray as we ought," then our very desire to pray as we should and our grief that we are not doing so shows that the Spirit is himself making effective intercession for us in our hearts (Romans 8:26ff.), which is as reassuring as it is mysterious, and as thrilling as it is amazing.

Fourth, we must *honor* our Father by serving his interests. The center of our concern must be "thy name . . . kingdom . . . will," and we must be like good children in human families, ready to obey instructions.

Fifth, we must love our *brothers*, by constant care and prayer for them. The Lord's Prayer schools us in intercession for the family's needs: "Our Father . . . give us . . . forgive us . . . lead us . . . deliver us . . . ." "Us" means more than just me! For God's child, prayer is no "flight of the alone to the Alone," but concern for the family is built into it.

So we should be expressing faith in Christ, confidence in God, joy in the Holy Spirit, a purpose of obedience, and concern for our fellow Christians when we go to God and call him "Father." Only so shall we answer Jesus' intention in teaching us this form of address.

PRAISE AND THANKS

As invocation of God as Father opens this pattern prayer, so renewed realization of the family relationship—his parenthood, and our sonship by grace—should always come first in our practice of prayer. All right-minded praying starts with a long look Godward and a deliberate lifting up of one's heart to give thanks and adore, and it is just this to which "Father" calls us. Thanks for grace, and praise for God's paternity, and joy in our sonship and heirship should bulk large in Christian prayer, and if we never got beyond it we should still be praying to good purpose. First things first!

So I ask: Do we always pray to God as Father? And do we always praise when we pray?

FURTHER BIBLE STUDY

God's fatherhood:
- Romans 8:12-25
- Matthew 6:1-16

QUESTIONS FOR THOUGHT AND DISCUSSION

- What gives us the right to call God our Father? Why may only Christians do this?
- What is the importance of realizing our sonship to God when we pray?
- Why would one say, "The Lord's Prayer schools us in intercession for the family's needs"?

Thus says the One who is high and lifted up,
who inhabits eternity, whose name is Holy:
"I dwell in the high and holy place,
and also with him who is of a
contrite and lowly spirit. . . ."

ISAIAH 57:15

CHAPTER 4

Which Art in Heaven

The vitality of prayer lies largely in the vision of God that prompts it. Drab thoughts of God make prayer dull. (Could this be your problem?) A book was once published with the title *Great Prayers of the Bible*: the mark of great prayers, in the Bible or elsewhere, is that they express a great awareness of a great God.

The invocation of God in the Lord's Prayer draws us into just such an awareness. "Our Father" speaks of the quality and depth of God's love to Christ's people—all the sustained care and concern that a perfect father could show. "Who art in heaven" sets before us the fact that our divine Father is great—eternal, infinite, almighty: thus that phrase makes us realize that God's love is unchanging, unlimited, unconquerable in its purpose, and more than able to deal with all the needs we bring when we pray. Prayer shaped and supported by thoughts like this will not be dull.

HEAVEN

Since God is spirit, "heaven" here cannot signify a place remote from us that he inhabits. The Greek gods were thought of as spending most of their time far away from earth in the celestial equivalent of the Bahamas, but the God of the Bible is not like this. Granted, the "heaven" where saints and angels dwell has to be thought of as a sort of locality, because saints and angels, as God's creatures, exist in space and time; but when the Creator is said to be "in heaven," the thought is that he exists on a different *plane* from us, rather than in a different *place*. That God in heaven is always near to his children on earth is something that the Bible takes for granted throughout.

WORSHIP

Knowledge of God's greatness should both humble us (cut us down to size!) and move us to worship. The Lord's Prayer was meant to teach us, and not just to ask for things, but also to worship God for all that he is, and thus to *hallow his name* in our own hearts. Angels and saints in glory worship God as Father (Ephesians 3:14ff.), and so on earth must we.

*Though he is Lord of the worlds, he always has time
for us; his eye is on everything every moment, yet we
always have his full attention whenever we call on him.*

Knowing that our Father God is in heaven, or (putting
it the other way around) knowing that God in heaven is our
Father, is meant to increase our wonder, joy, and sense of
privilege at being his children and being given a hotline or
prayer for communication with him. Hotline it truly is, for
though he is Lord of the worlds, he always has time for us; his
eye is on everything every moment, yet we always have his
full attention whenever we call on him. Marvelous! But have
we really taken this in? It merits much thought, and there are
two roads along which our minds can travel in order to grasp
it properly.

Either: think first of God's greatness, as the infinite
and eternal Creator who "dwells in unapproachable light"
(1 Timothy 6:16), apparently remote. Think of Solomon's
question, "Will God indeed dwell with man on the earth?
Behold, heaven and the highest heaven cannot contain you"
(2 Chronicles 6:18). But then think of what is in effect God's
reply to Solomon: "Thus says the One who is high and lifted
up, who inhabits eternity, whose name is Holy: 'I dwell in the
high and holy place, and also with him who is of a contrite
and lowly spirit . . .'" (Isaiah 57:15). And then remind your-

self that this promise finds its deepest fulfillment when God becomes the Father of insignificant sinful mortals like us, sinners who are *contrite* in repentance and *humble* in acknowledging their ill-desert and fleeing by faith to Jesus for refuge. For this awesome, holy, transcendent God stoops down in love to lift us up from the gutter, so to speak, brings us into his family, gives himself to us in unstinting fellowship, and thus enriches us forever.

Or: think of God's fatherhood, and then remind yourself that he is "in heaven" (a "heavenly" Father, as we say), which means that he is free from all the limitations, inadequacies, and flaws that are found in earthly parents, and that his fatherhood, like all his other relationships, is from every standpoint absolutely ideal, perfect, and glorious. Dwell on the fact that there is no better father, no parent more deeply committed to his children's welfare, or more wise and generous in promoting it, than God the Creator.

Let your thoughts move to and fro like an accelerating pendulum, taking ever wider swings. "He's my Father—and he's God in heaven; he's God in heaven—and he's my Father! It's beyond belief—but it's true!" Grasp this, or rather, let it grasp you; then tell God what you feel about it; and that will be the worship that our Lord wanted to evoke when he gave us this thought-pattern for the invocation of the One who is both his Father and ours.

FURTHER BIBLE STUDY

In touch with the transcendent God:
• Isaiah 40

QUESTIONS FOR THOUGHT AND DISCUSSION

• What is the importance of the fact that the God to whom we pray is in heaven?
• What is meant by saying that God "exists on a different plane from us, rather than in a different place"? What does this tell us about God?
• What response should a knowledge of God's greatness evoke in us?

Not to us, O LORD,
but to your name give glory.

PSALM 115:1

CHAPTER 5

Hallowed Be
Thy Name

Were we left to ourselves, any praying we did would both start and end with ourselves, for our natural self-centeredness knows no bounds. Indeed, much pagan praying of this kind goes on among supposedly Christian people. But Jesus' pattern prayer, which is both crutch, road, and walking lesson for the spiritually lame like ourselves, tells us to start with God: for lesson one is to grasp that God matters infinitely more than we do. So "thy" is the keyword of the opening three petitions, and the first request of all is "hallowed [holy, sanctified] be *thy name*"—which is the biggest and most basic request of the whole prayer. Understand it and make it your own, and you have unlocked the secret of both prayer and life.

GLORY BE TO GOD

What does "hallowed be thy name" ask for? God's "name" in the Bible regularly means the *person* he has revealed himself to be. "Hallowed" means known, acknowledged, and honored as holy. "Holy" is the Bible word for all that makes God different from us, in particular his awesome power and purity. This petition, then, asks that the praise and honor of the God of the Bible, and of him only, should be the issue of everything.

The idea that "glory be to God alone" is a motto distinguishing John Calvin and his admirers is no discredit to them, but it is a condemning sideswipe at all other versions of Christianity. In truth, however, every school of Christian thought insists, more or less clearheadedly, that the praise of God, as distinct from the promoting of ourselves, is the proper purpose of man's life. "Not to us, O LORD, but to your name give glory" (Psalm 115:1).

A SENSE OF DIRECTION

Who can pray this request and mean it? Only he who looks at the whole of life from this point of view. Such a man will not fall into the trap of superspirituality, so concentrating on God's redemption as to disregard his creation; people like that, however devoted and well-meaning, are unearthly in more senses than one, and injure their own humanity. Instead, he will see everything as stemming ultimately from the Creator's hand, and therefore as fundamentally good and fascinating, whatever man may have made of it (beauty, sex, nature, children, arts, crafts, food, games, no less than theology and church things). Then in thankfulness and joy he will so live as to help others see life's values and praise God for them, as he does. Supremely in this drab age, hallowing God's name starts here, with an attitude of gratitude for the goodness of the creation.

But it does not stop here. Hallowing God's name requires praise for the goodness and greatness of his redemptive work too, with its dazzling blend of wisdom, love, justice, power, and faithfulness. By wisdom God found a way to justify the unjust justly; in love he gave his Son to bear death's agony for us; in justice he made the Son, as our substitute, suffer the sentence that our disobedience deserved; with power he unites us to the risen Christ, renews our hearts, frees us from sin's bondage, and moves us to repent and believe; and in faithfulness he keeps us from falling, as he promised to do (see John 10:28ff.; 1 Corinthians 1:7ff.; 1 Peter 1:3-9), till he brings us triumphantly to our final glory. We do not save ourselves! Neither the Father's saving grace, nor the Son's saving work, nor our own saving faith originate with us; all is God's gift. Salvation, first to last, is of the Lord, and the hallowing of God's name requires us to acknowledge this, and to praise and adore him for the whole of it.

By wisdom God found a way to justify the unjust justly; in love he gave his Son to bear death's agony for us; in justice he made the Son, as our substitute, suffer the sentence that our disobedience deserved; with power he unites us to the risen Christ, renews our hearts, frees us from sin's bondage, and moves us to repent and believe; and in faithfulness he keeps us from falling, as he promised to do, till he brings us triumphantly to our final glory.

Nor is this all. God's name is only fully hallowed when he is worshiped for ordering all things for his people's ultimate good (cf. Romans 8:28), and also for the truth and trustworthiness of his written Word, which every believer should prize as "a lamp to my feet and a light to my path" (Psalm 119:105). "You have exalted above all things your name and your word," says the psalmist (138:2, margin), and so responsively must we. God's name—meaning, God himself—is dishonored if his children live in fear, as if their Father had lost control of his world, or in uncertainty, as if they dare not follow their Elder Brother's example and receive the teaching and promises of the Bible as instruction from the Father himself. There is, unhappily, widespread failure today to hallow God's name in these ways.

The hallowing throughout is by *gratitude*; what dishonors

God is non-appreciation and lack of gratitude, which Paul pinpoints as the root cause of men's falling away from God (Romans 1:20ff.). It is by being, not merely knowledgeable but, grateful and by expressing gratitude in thankful obedience that we honor and glorify our Maker. "Hallowed be thy name" expresses the desire that we ourselves and all rational beings with us should give God glory in this way.

Scripture calls the spirit that hallows God's name the "fear" of the Lord, hereby signifying awe and esteem for God's majesty on the one hand and humble trust (yes, trust, not mistrust or scaredness!) on the other. A classic text here is Psalm 111. "Praise the LORD. . . . Great are the works of the LORD . . . full of splendor and majesty . . . faithful and just; all his precepts are trustworthy . . . he has commanded his covenant for ever. Holy and awesome is his name!" And then, "The fear of the LORD [the response of praise for God's works and words, which the psalm has been voicing] is the beginning of wisdom" (discernment of the way to live).

The old term of respect, "God-fearing" (rarely used today, perhaps because there are few to whom it would apply), normally carried the implication of good sense and mature humanity as well as that of godliness, and thus reflected our fathers' awareness that the two go together; true reverence for God's name leads to true wisdom, realistic and shrewd, and when Christians appear goofy and shallow one has to ask whether they have yet learned what the hallowing of God's name means.

MAN'S CHIEF END

"Man's chief end," says the Shorter Catechism magnificently, "is to glorify God, and to enjoy him for ever." "End," note, not "ends"; for the two activities are one. God's chief end, purposed in all that he does, is his glory (and what higher end could he have?), and he has so made us that we find our own deepest fulfillment and highest joy in hallowing his name by praise, submission, and service. God is no sadist, and the principle of our creation is that, believe it or not (and or course many don't, just as Satan doesn't), our duty, interest, and delight completely coincide.

Christians get so hung up with the pagan idea (very dishonoring to God, incidentally) that God's will is always unpleasant, so that one is rather a martyr to be doing it, that they hardly at first notice how their experience verifies the truth that in Christian living duty and delight go together. But they do! And this will be even clearer in the life to come. To give oneself to hallowing God's name as one's life-task means that living, though never a joyride, will become increasingly a joy *road*. Can you believe that? Well, the proof of the pudding is in the eating! Try it, and you will see.

FURTHER BIBLE STUDY

God's name glorified:

• Psalm 148

QUESTIONS FOR THOUGHT AND DISCUSSION

• How does the Lord's Prayer differ from prayers we would form if left to ourselves?

• In your own words, what does it mean to hallow God's name?

• How does the belief that all comes ultimately from God affect one's outlook on life?

"The time is fulfilled, and the kingdom of God is at hand; repent, and believe in the gospel."

MARK 1:15

CHAPTER 6

Thy Kingdom Come

That "the Lord is King" in the sense of being sovereign over his world is assumed throughout the Bible. But God's king*ship* and his king*dom* are different things. The former is a fact of creation, commonly called providence; the latter is a reality of redemption, properly called grace.

This distinction is biblical in substance, but the vocabulary of Scripture does not show it. *Kingdom* is used in both Testaments for both God's universal sovereign sway and his redemptive relationship to individuals through Jesus Christ. In the Lord's Prayer, "thy kingdom come" uses the word in the latter sense, "thine is the kingdom" in the former.

God in sovereignty overrules the lives and doings of all men, including those who deliberately defy and disobey him. In a monstrous outburst of sibling rivalry surpassed only by Cain's fratricide, Joseph's brothers sold him into slavery and told his father that Joseph was dead. Yet God was overruling, so that later Joseph could say, "You meant evil against me; but God meant it for good" (Genesis 50:20). "By the hands of lawless men" the Jews of Jerusalem "crucified and killed" Jesus; yet God was overruling, so that Jesus was "delivered up according to the definite plan and foreknowledge of God," and by his death the world was redeemed (Acts 2:23).

But this overruling is a different thing from God's reign of grace in the heart and life of one who bows in penitent trust before his authority, desiring only to be delivered from evil and led in paths of righteousness. And that is precisely how it is when we make Jesus king.

JESUS AND THE KINGDOM

So God's kingdom is not a place, but rather a relationship. It exists wherever people enthrone Jesus as Lord of their lives. When Jesus began preaching that "the kingdom of God is at hand" (literally, "has drawn near"), he meant that the long-promised enjoyment of God's salvation for which Israel had been waiting was now there for them to enter (Mark 1:15). How were they to enter it? The Gospels answer that question very fully. Why, by becoming Jesus' disciples; by giving him their hearts' loyalty, and letting him reshape their lives; by receiving forgiveness from him; by identifying with his concerns; by loving him without reserve, and giving his claims precedence over all others—in short, by manifesting what Paul called "faith working through love" (Galatians 5:6), faith that acknowledges and embraces Jesus Christ as, in Peter's phrase, "Lord and Savior" (2 Peter 1:11; 2:20; 3:2, 18).

To this faith Jesus pointed Nicodemus (John 3:13-15), having told him that no one sees or enters the kingdom without a radical inner transformation by the Spirit, which he pictured as being "born again" (vv. 3-8). The passage instructs us that none of us can enter the kingdom without the Spirit's help, and we must not be too proud to ask for it, nor refuse to be changed in whatever ways God sees necessary.

The kingdom arrived with Jesus; indeed, one might say that as Son of God incarnate, Jesus is the kingdom of God in person. His rule over Christians is regal in the full-blooded biblical sense, personal, direct, and absolute. His claims are the claims of God, overriding those of man. Yet his rule is not tyranny, for King Jesus is his people's servant, their shepherd and champion, ordering all things for their protection and enrichment. "My yoke is easy, and my burden is light" (Matthew 11:30).

Also, he is their brother in the royal family, who himself lived on earth as "a man under authority" (Matthew 8:9); he will not ask more of us than was asked of him; indeed, not so much. His rule has the nature, not of dictatorship, but of pastoral care. "I am the good shepherd; I know my own" (John 10:14).

Jesus' claims are the claims of God, overriding those of man. Yet his rule is not tyranny, for King Jesus is his people's servant, their shepherd and champion, ordering all things for their protection and enrichment.

The first and fundamental service rendered by "great David's greater Son" to his disciples is to save them from sin and death, according to God's promise. So the kingdom of God is the realm of grace, where the damage done to us by sin is repaired; and the gospel of grace proves to be what the kingdom is all about.

PRESENT AND FUTURE

In one sense, the kingdom is here now, and Christians are in it. But in another sense—that of perfecting the display of God's grace in this world—the kingdom remains future and awaits Christ's return. The prayer "thy kingdom come" looks on to that day. But this does not exhaust its meaning. Any request for a new display of God's sovereignty in grace—renewing the church, converting sinners, restraining evil, providing good in this world—is a further spelling out of "thy kingdom come." If one asks where in the Lord's Prayer does general intercession appear, the answer is here. (And if one asks, Why burden oneself with a load of intercession? the answer is, Because we are taught to pray, "Thy kingdom come.")

THE PERSONAL CHALLENGE

To pray "thy kingdom come" is searching and demanding, for one must be ready to add, "and start with me; make me your fully obedient subject. Show me my place among 'workers for the kingdom of God' (Colossians 4:11), and use me, so far as may be, to extend the kingdom and so be your means of answering my prayer." Made sincerely, this is a prayer that the Savior who calls us to self-denial and cross-bearing and consent that one's life be lost, one way or another, in serving the gospel may have his way with us completely. Do we really seek this? Have we faced it? Let every man examine himself, and so—only so—let him say the Lord's Prayer.

FURTHER BIBLE STUDY

The kingdom of God (=heaven):
• Matthew 13:1-52

QUESTIONS FOR THOUGHT AND DISCUSSION

- Do you agree that "God's kingdom is not a place, but a relationship"? Why or why not?
- Why can we rightly say that Jesus was (and is) a king but not a tyrant?
- Think out the present-day implications of the prayer "thy kingdom come," so far as you are able to see them.

"My Father, if it be possible,
let this cup pass from me;
nevertheless, not as I will,
but as you will."

MATTHEW 26:39

CHAPTER 7

Thy Will Be Done

Every word of the Lord's Prayer reflects the Lord's vision of what our lives should be—unified, all-embracing response to the love of our heavenly Father, so that we seek his glory, trust his care, and obey his word every moment of every day. If, therefore, we are to pray the Lord's Prayer with understanding and sincerity, we must make this vision our own. So when I say "hallowed be thy name; thy kingdom come," I should be adding in my mind the words "in and through me," and so giving myself to God afresh to be, so far as I can be, the means of answering my own prayer. And when I say "thy will be done," I should mean this as a prayer that I, along with the rest of God's people, may learn to be obedient.

Here more clearly than anywhere the purpose of prayer becomes plain: not to make God do my will (which is practicing magic), but to bring my will into line with his (which is what it means to practice true religion).

NOT MY WILL

So understood, "thy will be done" takes some praying! I cannot sincerely ask for the doing of God's will without denying myself, for when we get down to the business of everyday living, we regularly find that it is our will rather than his that we want to do, or to see happening. Nor can I pray this prayer without dedicating myself to keep loyal to God in face of all the opposition that in this fallen world, where Satan is "prince" (John 14:30, JB, NEB), I regularly meet. Luther expounded the words like this: "Let thy will be done, O Father, not the will of the devil, or of any of those who would overthrow thy holy Word or hinder the coming of thy kingdom; and grant that all we may have to endure for its sake may be borne with patience and overcome, so that our poor flesh may not yield or give way from weakness or laziness." For God's will to be done in our lives *on earth* in the way that it is done among the angels will involve us in quite a struggle.

See what this petition meant when Jesus voiced it in Gethsemane (Matthew 26:39, 42). The incarnate Lord was in the grip of mind-blowing horror, evoked not just by the expectation of physical pain and outward disgrace (strong men can bear these things in a good cause without too much ado), but by the prospect of being *made sin* and forsaken by his Father on the cross. "Never man feared death like this man," said Luther truly; and this was why. His whole being shrank from it; yet his prayer remained, "not as I will, but as you will" (vv. 39, 42). What it cost him to pray thus we shall never know. What it may cost us to accept God's will we cannot say either—which is, perhaps, as well.

ACCEPTING GOD'S WILL

The Greek for "be done," in both the Lord's Prayer and the Gethsemane story, literally means "happen," and God's will here is two things—his purpose for events and his command to his people. In relation to the former, "thy will be done" expresses the spirit of meekness, which accepts without complaining whatever God sends, or fails to send. In relation to the latter, we are asking God to teach us all that we should do and make us both willing and able for the task. Can you pray this from the heart? It is not so easy as it looks.

FINDING GOD'S WILL

But how shall we know what God wants of us? By paying attention to his Word and to our own consciences, by noting what circumstances allow, and by taking advice in order to check our own sense of the situation and the adequacy of our insight into what is right. Problems about God's will regularly come clear as they are bounced off other Christian minds. One's own inner state is important too. "If anyone's will is to do God's will," not only will he know that Jesus and his teaching are from God (John 7:17), but he will be told if he is out of the way. "Your ears shall hear a word behind you, saying, 'This is the way, walk in it,' when you turn to the right or when you turn to the left" (Isaiah 30:21). If you are open to God, God will get through to you with the guidance you need. That is a promise!

"O Lord God, Holy Father, who has called us through Christ to be partakers of this gracious Covenant, we take upon ourselves with joy the yoke of obedience, and engage ourselves, for love of Thee, to see and do thy perfect will."

When you are unclear as to God's will, wait if you can; if you have to act, make what you think is the best decision, and God will soon let you know if you are not on the right track.

A COVENANT WITH GOD

Here, in closing, are some extracts from the superb Covenant Service of the Methodist Church, which say exactly what you and I should now be saying. Following a reminder that in the New Covenant God promises us "all that he declared in Jesus Christ," while we for our part "stand pledged to live no more unto ourselves," the leader says:

> O Lord God, Holy Father, who has called us through Christ to be partakers of this gracious Covenant, we take upon ourselves with joy the yoke of obedience, and engage ourselves, for love of Thee, to see and do thy perfect will.

Then all the worshipers join in words that John Wesley took from the Puritan Richard Alleine for this purpose in 1755:

> I am no longer my own, but Thine. Put me to what Thou wilt, rank me with whom Thou wilt; put me to doing, put me to suffering; let me be employed for Thee or laid aside for Thee, exalted for Thee or brought low for Thee; let me be full, let me be empty; let me have all things, let me have nothing; I freely and heartily yield all things to Thy pleasure and disposal.
>
> And now, O glorious and blessed God, Father, Son and Holy Spirit, Thou art mine, and I am Thine. So be it. And the Covenant which I have made on earth, let it be ratified in heaven. Amen.

FURTHER BIBLE STUDY

The will of God:
• Acts 20:16–21:14

QUESTIONS FOR THOUGHT AND DISCUSSION

- What is prayer's true purpose? Is this why you pray?
- What does prayer have to do with denying ourselves?
- What are some of the problems involved in finding God's will for our lives, and how should we deal with them?

*"Your will be done,
on earth as it is in heaven."*

MATTHEW 6:10

CHAPTER 8

On Earth As It Is in Heaven

Three doctrinal statements bind the Lord's Prayer together. The first two come in the invocation. God is the Father of Christian people, and he is in heaven. The third rounds off the first trio of petitions: in heaven God's will is done. The first proclaims God's goodness in redeeming us through the cross and taking us into his family. The second and third declare his greatness and power to achieve his purpose. Together, these three truths point up the Christian hope. As our Father, God stands pledged to love us and do us good for all eternity.

HEAVEN

As Lord of creation, ruling in heaven, i.e., in freedom from the limitations of space-time creaturehood here on earth, God can be relied on to fulfill his intention perfectly. You and I are capable of failing in anything we undertake, however simple, but it is God's glory to succeed in all that he has set himself to do, however hard. So

The work which his mercy began
The arm of his strength will complete;
His promise is yea and amen,
And never was forfeited yet.

Things future, nor things that are now,
Not all things below or above,
Can make him his purpose forego,
Nor sever my soul from his love.

But when Jesus says that in heaven God's will is done, he is not thinking so much of our Father's transcendence as of a community of created beings, intelligent like ourselves, living nearer to God (in the sense that they enjoy more of him than we can in this world), and serving him with an ecstatic whole-heartedness that in this life we never attain. This is "heaven" in the most usual sense of the word, the "heaven" to which Christians "go" when they die, the state of life for which our time here is all preparation and training.

Heaven in this sense is infinitely more important than the present life, not only because it is endless while this life is temporary, but also because no relationships are perfectly enjoyed here in the way that they will be hereafter. From the fact that the

Holy Trinity is the ultimate reality, no less than from the insights of present-day psychologists, we learn that relationships are what life—real life, as distinct from mere consciousness—is really all about, and relationships, with Father, Son, and saints, are certainly what heaven is all about. It is no accident that the New Testament presents heaven as a city (Revelation 21), a banquet (Matthew 8:11; Luke 22:29ff.; Revelation 19:9), and a worshiping congregation (Hebrews 12:22-24; cf. Revelation 7:9-17). These pictures are telling us that heaven will be an experience of *togetherness*, closer and more joyous than any we have known so far, whether with our God or with our fellow-believers.

In *The Great Divorce*, C. S. Lewis imagines hell as a country where people are always scattering to get as far from each other as they can! (And Sartre in *No Exit* pictured hell as other people from whom one can never get away, however hellishly they behave.) But in heaven the saints will be close to each other, as well as to the Father and the Son—and glad to be; and the closeness will add to the joy.

Heaven will be an experience of togetherness, closer and more joyous than any we have known so far, whether with our God or with our fellow-believers.

With robust emphasis, Scripture is other-worldly, insisting that the life of heaven is better and more glorious than life on earth at every point. But when we ask just how, Scripture says to us in effect, "Wait and see (cf. Romans 8:24); and realize that it is so far beyond your present experience that you really can't conceive it." Heaven, being an order of reality not bounded by space and time as we know them, is not located in, nor can be defined by, this present world in which our physical nature anchors us. All we are sure of is that, as we said, for heaven's inhabitants (the "ministering spirits" who are angels, with "the spirits of just men made perfect") it is a state of perfect communion with God, and with others in God, and complete contentment in his presence. That is the further truth the Bible pictures of the golden city and the great feast are meant to convey.

But for perfect communion not only must God give without limit or restraint; his servants, angelic and human, must also respond without reserve—which means that in and through them God's will is fully done. The doing of God's will is thus part of the definition of heaven, and it is part of heaven's glory that God gives those who are there full ability to do it.

PRAISE

Why did Jesus follow "thy will be done on earth" with "as it is in heaven"? Surely for two reasons.

First, he wants at this point to arouse *hope*. The chaos

of earth mocks the petition; by reminding us, however, that God has already established his will perfectly in heaven, Jesus stirs us to hope that on earth we may yet see great things. "Is anything too hard for the LORD?" (Genesis 18:14).

Nor is this all. Jesus' second aim is to awaken *praise*. While petition exhausts, praise invigorates, and for Jesus to interpose between two spells of arduous petition a moment to pause and praise—"in heaven, Father, your will is done! hallelujah!"—is the spiritual equivalent of refreshment at half-time, whereby strength for the battle of intercession is renewed. Here Jesus teaches the precious lesson that *praising energizes and renews praying.* Hear him!

FURTHER BIBLE STUDY

Earth and heaven:
• Hebrews 12

QUESTIONS FOR THOUGHT AND DISCUSSION

• What is the significance of God's not being limited by space and time?
• What are the necessary elements of perfect communion with God?
• What is meant by the phrase "while petition exhausts, praise invigorates"?

"Seek first the kingdom of God and his righteousness, and all these things will be added to you."

MATTHEW 6:33

CHAPTER 9

Our Daily Bread

Having focused on God's name, kingdom, and will, the Lord's Prayer turns attention to our meals. Is this a let-down? Not at all: it is a genuine progression. How so?

Firstly, those who truly pray the first three petitions thereby commit themselves to live wholly for God, and the natural and logical next request is for food to give them energy for this. Dr. Johnson's reply to the criticism that he cared much for his stomach was that those who ignore the needs of their stomach are soon in no condition to care about anything else. Christian realism? Yes, just that.

Secondly, we do in fact depend every moment on our Father-Creator to keep us and the rest of the universe in being (for without his will nothing could still exist), and to sustain nature's rhythmical functioning so that each year sees seedtime, harvest, and food in the shops (cf. Genesis 8:22). And it is right for us to acknowledge this dependence regularly in prayer, particularly in an age like ours that, having assumed nature to be self-sustaining, now has problems about the reality of God.

Some regard petitions for personal material needs as low-grade prayer, as if God were not interested in the physical side of life and we should not be either. But such hyper-spirituality is really an unspiritual ego trip; see how in Colossians 2:23 Paul warns that man-made asceticism does not stop indulgence of the flesh (i.e., the sinful self). Petitions looking to God as the sole and omnicompetent source of supply of all human needs, down to the most mundane, are expressing truth, and as the denying of our own self-sufficiency humbles us, so the acknowledging of our dependence honors God. Neither our minds nor our hearts are right till we see that it is as necessary and important to pray for daily bread as for (say) the forgiveness of sins.

Thirdly, God really is concerned that his servants should have the food they need, as Jesus' feedings of the 4,000 and 5,000 show. God cares about physical needs no less than spiritual; to him, the basic category is that of *human* needs, comprising both.

THE BODY

This petition shows us how to regard our bodies. The Christian way is not to deify them, making health and beauty ends in themselves, as modern pagans do; nor is it to despise them, making scruffiness a virtue, as some ancient pagans (and Christians too, unfortunately) once did. It is rather to accept one's body as part of God's good creation, to act as its steward and manager, and gratefully to enjoy it as one does so. Thus we honor its Maker. Such enjoyment is in no way unspiritual for Christ's disciples; for them, it is like their salvation, the Lord's free gift.

The Bible opposes all long-faced asceticism by saying that if you enjoy health, good appetite, physical agility, and marriage in the sense that you have been given them, you should enjoy them in the further sense of delighting in them. Such delight is (not the whole, but) part of our duty and our service of God, for without it we are being simply ungrateful for good gifts. As Screwtape truly said (with disgust), "He's a hedonist at heart": God values pleasure, and it is his pleasure to give pleasure. Well did some rabbis teach that at the judgment God will hold against us every pleasure that he offered us and we neglected. Do we yet know how to enjoy ourselves—yes, physically too—to the glory of God?

MATERIAL NEEDS

Note that we are to pray for "*our* daily bread." There is intercession for other Christians here as well as petition for oneself. And "bread," man's staple diet in both the ancient and the modern worlds, stands here for all of life's necessities and the means of supplying them. Thus, "bread" covers all food; so the prayer is for farmers and against famine. Again, the prayer covers clothing, shelter, and physical health; so the prayer becomes an intercession for social and medical services. Or again, the prayer covers money and power to earn, and so becomes a cry against poverty, unemployment, and national policies that produce or prolong both. Luther wished that rulers put loaves rather than lions in their coats of arms, to remind themselves that their people's welfare must come first, and he urged that it is under this clause of the Lord's Prayer that prayer for those in authority most properly comes.

DAILY

J. B. Phillips correctly rendered this clause, "give us this (each) day the bread we need." We are told to ask for bread, as the Israelites were told to gather manna, on a day-to-day basis: the Christian way is to live in constant dependence on God, a day at a time. Also, we are to ask for the bread we *need*; i.e., for the supply of necessities, not luxuries we can do without. This petition does not sanctify greed! Moreover, we must as we pray be prepared to have God show us, by his providential response of not giving what we sought, that we did not really need it after all.

We are to ask for the bread we need; i.e., for the supply of necessities, not luxuries we can do without. This petition does not sanctify greed!

Now comes the real test of faith. You, the Christian, have (I assume) prayed for today's bread. Will you now believe that what comes to you, much or little, is God's answer, according to the promise of Matthew 6:33? And will you on that basis be content with it, and grateful for it? Over to you.

FURTHER BIBLE STUDY

God provides:
- Psalm 104
- Matthew 6:19-34

QUESTIONS FOR THOUGHT AND DISCUSSION

- Do you agree that God is as concerned about physical needs as he is about spiritual ones? Why or why not?
- As good stewards, what attitudes should we have toward our own bodies?
- Why, and in what sense, is Christianity meant to be a day-at-a-time life?

"For if you forgive others their trespasses, your heavenly Father will also forgive you; but if you do not forgive others their trespasses, neither will your Father forgive your trespasses."

MATTHEW 6:14, 15

CHAPTER 10

Forgive Us

The Christian lives through forgiveness. This is what justification by faith is all about. We could have no life or hope with God at all, had God's Son not borne the penalty of our sins so that we might go free. But Christians fall short still, and forgiveness is needed each day; so Jesus in part two of his model prayer included a request for it between the pleas for material provision and spiritual protection. This reflects nothing in his own praying, for he knew he was sinless (cf. John 8:46); it is here for us.

DEBTS

How should Christians see their sins? Scripture presents sins as lawbreaking, deviation, shortcoming, rebellion, pollution (dirt), and missing one's target, and it is always all these things in relation to God; but the special angle from which the Lord's Prayer views it is that of unpaid debts. "Forgive us our debts, as we also have forgiven our debtors" is the RSV rendering of Matthew 6:12 (see also Luke 11:4 and the parable of the two debtors, Matthew 18:23ff.). Those denominations that say "trespasses" instead of "debts," echoing Luke 11:4 (in some translations), unfortunately miss this point. Jesus' thought is that we owe God total, tireless loyalty—zealous love for God and men, all day and every day, on the pattern of Jesus' own—and our sin is basically failure to pay. The Anglican Prayer Book rightly confesses sins of omission ("we have left undone those things which we ought to have done") before sins of commission: the omission perspective is basic. When Christians examine themselves, it is for omissions that they should first look, and they will always find that their saddest sins take the form of good left undone. When the dying Archbishop Ussher prayed, "Lord, forgive most of all my sins of omission," he showed a true sense of spiritual reality.

SINNING SONS

A problem arises here. If Christ's death atoned for all sins, past, present, and future (as it did), and if God's verdict justifying the believer ("I accept you as righteous for Jesus' sake") is eternally valid (as it is), why need the Christian mention his daily sins to God at all? The answer lies in distinguishing between God as Judge and as Father, and between being a justified sinner and an adopted son. The Lord's Prayer is the family prayer, in which God's adopted children address their Father, and though their daily failures do not overthrow their justification, things will not be right between them and their Father till they have said, "Sorry" and asked him to overlook the ways they have let him down. Unless Christians come to God each time as returning prodigals, their prayer will be as unreal as was that of the Pharisee in Jesus' parable.

> *The Lord's Prayer is the family prayer, in which*
> *God's adopted children address their Father, and*
> *though their daily failures do not overthrow their*
> *justification, things will not be right between them*
> *and their Father till they have said, "Sorry" and asked*
> *him to overlook the ways they have let him down.*

INTOLERABLE

Here emerges a lesson: Christians must be willing to examine themselves and let others examine them for the detecting of day-to-day shortcomings. The Puritans valued preachers who would "rip up" the conscience; more such preaching is needed today. The discipline of self-examination, though distasteful to our pride, is necessary because our holy Father in heaven will not turn a blind eye to his children's failings, as human parents so often (and so unwisely) do. So what he knows about our sins we need to know too, so that we may repent and ask pardon for whatever has given offense.

From one standpoint, Christians' shortcomings offend most of all just because they have most reason (the love of God in Christ) and most resources (the indwelling Holy Spirit) for avoiding sinful ways. Those who think that because in Christ their sins are covered they need not bother to keep God's law are desperately confused (see Romans 6). As it upsets a man more to learn that his wife is sleeping around than that the girl next door is doing it, so God is most deeply outraged when his own people are unfaithful (see Hosea's prophecy, especially chapters 1–3). "This is the will of God, your sanctification" (1 Thessalonians 4:3)—and nothing less will do.

The Communion Service in the 1662 Prayer Book teaches Christians to call the "burden" (guilt) of their sins "intolerable." The justification for this strong language is knowledge of the intolerable grief brought to God by the sins of his own family. How sensitive are we to this? And how concerned that, as sons of God, our lives should be so far as possible sin-free? The true Christian will not only seek to find and face his sins through self-examination, but he will labor "by the Spirit" to "put to death the deeds of the body" (i.e., the habits of the old sinful self) all his days (Romans 8:13).

Only the Forgiving are Forgiven

Those who hope for God's forgiveness, said Jesus, must be able to tell him that they too have forgiven their debtors. This is not a matter of earning forgiveness by works, but of qualifying for it by repentance. Repentance—change of mind—makes mercy and forbearance central to one's new lifestyle. Those who live by God's forgiveness must imitate it; one whose only hope is that God will not hold his faults against him forfeits his right to hold others' faults against them. "Do as you would be done by" is the rule here, and the unforgiving Christian brands himself a hypocrite. It is true that forgiveness is by faith in Christ alone, apart from works, but repentance is faith's fruit, and there is no more reality in a profession of faith than there is reality of repentance accompanying it. Jesus himself stresses that only those who grant forgiveness will receive it in Matthew 6:14ff.; 18:35.

So again the question is: can I say the Lord's Prayer? Can you? We shall all do well to make the following lines a plea of our own:

"Forgive our sins as we forgive,"
—you taught us, Lord, to pray;
But you alone can grant us grace
To live the words we say.

How can your pardon reach
*   and bless*
The unforgiving heart
That broods on wrongs,
*   and will not let*
Old bitterness depart?

In blazing light your Cross reveals
The truth we dimly knew,
How small the debts men owe to us,
How great our debt to you.

Lord, cleanse the depths within
*   our souls,*
And bid resentment cease;
Then, reconciled to God and man,
Our lives will spread your peace.

FURTHER BIBLE STUDY

Asking forgiveness:
• Psalm 51
Qualifying for forgiveness:
• Matthew 18:23-35

QUESTIONS FOR THOUGHT AND DISCUSSION

- How does the Lord's Prayer define sin? How is this seen in our daily living?
- Why does a person need to confess daily sins after he becomes a Christian?
- Why can unforgiving Christians rightly be called hypocrites?

*No temptation has overtaken you
that is not common to man. God is faithful,
and he will not let you be tempted beyond
your ability, but with the temptation he
will also provide the way of escape,
that you may be able to endure it.*

1 CORINTHIANS 10:13

CHAPTER 11

Not into Temptation

After prayer for provender and pardon comes a cry for protection, our third basic need. The sentence has two halves: "lead us not into temptation, but deliver us from evil" (either sin or trouble or both, or "the evil one" who manipulates trouble to induce sin). Both halves, however, express a single thought: "Life is a spiritual minefield; amid such dangers we dare not trust ourselves; Father, keep us safe." Here the Lord's Prayer links up with the view of life that runs through the Psalms. The realism, self-distrust, and humble dependence on God that breathes through this petition is something we all need to learn.

TESTING

The thought that God may lead Christians into temptation, as the first clause assumes, has puzzled and shocked many people. Things grow clearer, however, once we see what temptation means here. "Test" or "trial"—that is, a situation that reveals how far you are able to go right and avoid going wrong—is the idea behind the word. The driving test, which (believe it or not) is designed to enable you to show that you can do everything right, is a "temptation" in this sense. Now, any educational or training program must of necessity include periodic tests for gauging progress, and the experience of taking and passing such tests can be very encouraging to the trainee. In God's program for the spiritual education and growth of Christians, the same applies. God does and must test us regularly, to prove what is in us and to show how far we have come. His purpose in this is wholly constructive, to strengthen us and help us forward. Thus he "tested" Abraham (so ESV; AV has "tempt," RV "prove") by telling him to sacrifice Isaac, and after the test promised him great blessing "because you have obeyed my voice" (Genesis 22:1, 18).

NO PICNIC

Why, then, if temptation is beneficial, should we ask to be spared it? For three reasons. First, whenever God tests us for our good, Satan, "the tempter" (Matthew 4:3; 1 Thessalonians 3:5), tries to exploit the situation for our ruin. "Your adversary the devil prowls around like a roaring lion, seeking someone to devour" (1 Peter 5:8). Jesus knew from his wilderness experience how mean and cunning Satan is, and wished no one to underestimate him or to court a meeting with him. (Our modern occultists would do well to take this to heart.)

Second, the pressures in times of trial can be so appalling that no sane Christian can do other than shrink from them, just as they shrink from the thought of having cancer. For both reasons Jesus was as right to start his prayer in Gethsemane with "Father, remove this cup" as he was to end it with "yet not my will but yours be done" (cf. Matthew 26:39). Temptation is no picnic!

Third, knowledge of our own proven weakness, thick-headedness, and all-around vulnerability in spiritual matters, and of the skill with which Satan exploits our strong and weak points alike, mixing frontal assaults on our Christian integrity with tactics of infiltration and ambush, so that while avoiding one hazard we constantly fall victim to another, compels us to cry, in humility and self-distrust, "Lord, if it be possible, *please*, no temptation! I don't want to risk damaging myself and dishonoring you by falling!" Temptation may be our lot, but only a fool will make it his preference; others will heed Paul's warning to the spiritually reckless: "let any one who thinks that he stands take heed lest he fall" (1 Corinthians 10:12).

WATCH AND PRAY

When Jesus found his disciples asleep in Gethsemane, he said, "Watch and pray that you may not enter into [that is, start yielding to] temptation; the spirit indeed is willing [to do God's will], but the flesh [human nature] is weak" (Matthew 26:41). What prompted his comment was the struggle he had just had with himself, in which his own flesh had violently recoiled from the prospect of Calvary, plus now the sleep of those who, though tired, had been asked to watch with him—stay awake, that is, and support him by their presence and prayers. We must appreciate that the test of sincerity and realism in saying "lead us not into temptation" is readiness to "watch and pray," lest we fall victim to it unawares.

"Watch" suggests a soldier on guard, alert for the first signs of enemy attack. We *watch* against temptation by noting what situation, company, and influences expose us to it, and avoiding them whenever we can. As Luther said, you can't keep the birds from flying over your head, but you can keep them from nesting in your hair. Find out what for you is fire, and don't play with it!

We watch against temptation by noting what situation, company, and influences expose us to it, and avoiding them whenever we can.

"Pray" points to the kind of prayer Jesus had just made—prayer for strength to do what one knows is right in the face of inward reluctance plus any number of siren-songs seeking to charm one off course and spiritually onto the rocks.

Nobody ever expressed the right state of mind in this matter better than Charles Wesley, in the hymn that starts, "Jesus, my strength, my hope, on thee I cast my care."

> *I want a godly fear,*
> *A quick-discerning eye*
> *That looks to thee when sin is near*
> *And sees the tempter fly;*
> *A spirit still prepared*
> *And armed with jealous care,*
> *For ever standing on its guard*
> *And watching unto prayer.*

The conclusion of the matter is this. For good and necessary reasons connected with our Christian growth (cf. James 1:2-12), we shall not be spared all temptation (cf. 1 Corinthians 10:13). But if we ask to be spared and watch and pray against Satan's attempts to exploit situations for our downfall, we shall be tempted less than we might have been (cf. Revelation 3:10), and will find ourselves able to cope with temptation when it comes (1 Corinthians 10:13). So do not be unrealistic in not budgeting for temptation, nor foolhardy enough to court it; but when it comes, do not doubt God's power to deliver from the evil it brings, and to "keep you from stumbling" (Jude 24) as you pick your way through it. When you are not conscious of temptation, pray "lead us not into temptation," and when you are conscious of it, pray "deliver us from evil," and you will live.

FURTHER BIBLE STUDY

Eve's temptation:
• Genesis 3:1-7
Abraham's temptation:
• Genesis 22:1-19
Jesus' temptation:
• Luke 4:1-15

QUESTIONS FOR THOUGHT AND DISCUSSION

• What is temptation, as the word is used in the Lord's Prayer?
• What is God's purpose in testing us? How do you respond to such testing?
• Why should we ask to be spared from temptation?

"Watch and pray that you may not enter into temptation. The spirit indeed is willing, but the flesh is weak."

MATTHEW 26:41

CHAPTER 12

Deliver Us

The vision of life in God's family that we learn from the Lord's Prayer has three dimensions. It is a life of devotion, of dependence, and of danger. "Deliver us from evil" is a plea for protection in the face of danger that threatens—dangers that appear throughout the New Testament as constantly threatening the Christian believer.

DANGER

In our comfortable routines of life we do not think of ourselves as being in danger. But we should, for we are. Once more, the Anglican Prayer Book provides much insight. Thus, the Litany expands "deliver us from evil" into five distinct petitions, and among the evils specified, side by side with circumstantial troubles, are these:

> From sin, from the crafts and assaults of the devil . . . from all blindness of heart; from pride, vain-glory and hypocrisy; from

envy, hatred, and malice, and all uncharitableness . . . from for-
nication, and all other deadly sin; and from all the deceits of the
world, and flesh, and the devil . . . from sudden [unexpected,
and unprepared-for] death . . . from hardness of heart, and con-
tempt of thy Word and Commandment, *Good Lord, deliver us.*

Now we see what our deepest dangers are, and whence they
arise. The deliverance we need is not only or mainly from
adverse circumstances, but from the spiritual evil within
us that makes both adverse and favorable circumstances its
springboard for attack. Sin in our hearts, spawning all kinds
of inclinations to do something other than God's will and to
love something or someone more than God himself, is the
source of our danger. Always and everywhere, the danger of
being led astray by indwelling sin remains.

*The deliverance we need is not only or mainly from
adverse circumstances, but from the spiritual evil
within us that makes both adverse and favorable
circumstances its springboard for attack.*

DECEIT

Look again at the extract quoted from the Litany. All the evils
listed flow spontaneously from the fallen human heart. Satan
may be their ringmaster, deciding in what order they shall
come on for their performance, but he does not have to inject
them into our system; they are already there. And sin works

for the most part by deceit. "Blindness . . . deceits . . . hardness of heart" are the key words on sin's methods, as "pride . . . hypocrisy . . . uncharitableness" are the key words on sin's manifestations. But pride and uncharitableness will masquerade as zeal for God, his truth, and his church—and other moral and spiritual evils will regularly creep in unnoticed while our attention is on something else. This is the way of what a Puritan called "the mystery of self-deceiving," and what Hebrews calls "the deceitfulness of sin" (Hebrews 3:13).

Facing danger, sensible men keep cool but go carefully, keeping alert, watching each step and ready to cry "help" at the first sign of trouble. So too the sensible Christian will "watch and pray," lest he enter into temptation (see Matthew 26:41), and the cry for deliverance from evil will often be on his lips. And then he will be kept safe.

DELIVERANCE

The television program *This Is Your Life* reviewed each guest's personal history from the outside, in terms of work done and friends made. But if you were asked, "What is your life?" you would speak from the inside and go deeper. As a human being, you are a creature of purpose, and you would willy-nilly describe your life in terms of goals you have had and of challenges, conflicts, frustrations, and progress in pursuit of them.

The secular, man-centered way of doing this is by estimating achievement and non-achievement, success and failure in tasks tackled. Memoirs and biographies of public figures review their careers in this way. Bible writers, Bible characters, and biblical Christians, however, do differently.

To start with, they look at their lives God-centeredly. They see God as the one whose action has been the decisive factor shaping their lives, and as the only one who is able to assess what they have achieved. And they see his action in terms of two main concepts. The first is *mercy*: their lives appear to them as, in the words of the hymn, "mercy from first to last." The second concept is *deliverance*: they see themselves as having been delivered over and over again from trouble and opposition that threatened to keep them from, or obstruct them in, God's service and their fellowship with him. God "delivered us from such a deadly peril [affliction in Asia], and he will deliver us. On him we have set our hope that he will deliver us again" (2 Corinthians 1:10). So spoke Paul, and his sentiment is typical of the whole biblical view of life, according to which hope for mercy and deliverance from evil, sin within and storms without, is an essential element in faith at all times. A little time with a concordance exploring the Bible uses of *deliver* and *deliverance* will convince you of this.

Can you yet see your own life in terms of being threatened and endangered by evil of all sorts, and so of needing

God's deliverance every moment? If not, believe me, you cannot yet see what you are looking at! You are like a person wandering blindfolded and with ears plugged in the middle of a city street, with traffic coming both ways. Learn from the Lord's Prayer what is really going on in your life, and as you are increasingly enabled to discern the dangers, lean harder on the Great Deliverer. "Because he holds fast to me in love, I will deliver him"—that is God's promise to each saint (Psalm 91:14). Claim it; it is for you.

FURTHER BIBLE STUDY

A song of deliverance:
• 2 Samuel 22 (= Psalm 18)

QUESTIONS FOR THOUGHT AND DISCUSSION

• What does the fact that we must regularly pray for spiritual protection tell us about our lives?
• What is meant by the phrase "the spiritual evil within us that makes both adverse and favorable circumstances its springboard for attack"?
• What is meant by the Puritan phrase, "the mystery of self-deceiving"?

[Christ] disarmed the rulers and authorities and put them to open shame, by triumphing over them in him.

COLOSSIANS 2:15

CHAPTER 13

From Evil

The first thing to say about evil is that it is a reality, and we should not pretend that there is no such thing. Christian Scientists, like Hindu mystics, want to think it away as an illusion; others would see it as good in the making, or good misunderstood. But in the Bible evil is as real as good, and the distinction between them is ultimate.

The second thing to say about evil is that it is an irrational and meaningless reality, making no sense, and only definable as good perverted.

The third thing to say about evil is that God is handling it. At the cost of Calvary he has taken responsibility for bringing good out of it; already he has triumphed over it, and eventually he will eliminate it. The Christian contemplating evil is not a pessimist, for he knows that one day this mad and meaningless reality that destroys good shall be destroyed itself. Christ ensured this by conquering cosmic evil on the cross (see Colossians 2:15); he will finally snuff it out at his return.

On that day the Christian expects to see that out of all his embroilments with the evil in and around him has come greater good for him, and greater glory for God, than could have been otherwise. That will finally vindicate the goodness and wisdom of God in giving evil so long a run in his world.

TWO SORTS OF EVIL

Evil means badness that has the effect of ruining, or wasting, or ruling out, goodness—that is, the achieving of a life that is upright, worthwhile, and joyful. Evil, as defined, takes two forms. First, there is badness external to us, the badness of circumstances, "trouble, sorrow, need, sickness, or any other adversity." Circumstances become evil when they inflict on us more pain and frustration than we can turn into good by the way that we take them. In fact, circumstances are not often that bad. Beethoven was able to turn the frustration of deafness and the pain of loneliness into the music of hero-ism; countless invalids have been able to achieve dignity and serenity despite chronic physical agony; and the psalmist can say, "It is good for me that I was afflicted, that I might learn your statutes" (Psalm 119:71). Yet when, as sometimes happens, pain is such that a man can only scream till he faints from exhaustion, this is surely evil.

Second, there is badness within us, the badness of corruption. This is the badness of bad men and fallen angels, the badness that is from one standpoint a lack of good and from another good gone wrong: as in the devil, in Adam, and in you and me. How and why good corrupts, goes wrong, is more than Scripture explains or than we can grasp, but the fact is there. And whereas in relation to the first sort of evil we are passive, suffering it, in relation to the second sort we are active, doing it. "The evil I do not want is what I keep on doing," says Paul (Romans 7:19); to which every honest man's response must be, "Yes, and so do I."

GOD TO THE RESCUE

Christians cannot disregard evil around and within them, nor are they at liberty to try, for their calling is to face evil and overcome it with good (Romans 12:21). But this assumes that evil does not overcome them; and here the Lord's Prayer comes in once more.

Jesus tells us to ask God to "deliver us from evil." Whether this Greek phrase means "evil" in general (so ESV text) or "the evil one" (so ESV margin) does not matter, though the second is perhaps likelier. The first rendering would mean "deliver us from all the evil in the world, in ourselves, in other men, in Satan and his hosts." The second rendering would mean "deliver us from Satan, who seeks our ruin, and from all that he exploits to that end—all the ungodliness of the world, all the sinfulness of our flesh, all spiritual evil of every sort." Both renderings come to the same thing.

Christians cannot disregard evil around and within them, nor are they at liberty to try, for their calling is to face evil and overcome it with good.

And the great point is that Jesus' act of giving us this prayer is an implicit promise that if we seek deliverance from evil, we shall find it. The moment we cry "deliver," God's rescue operation will start; help will be on the way to cope with whatever form of evil threatens us.

FURTHER BIBLE STUDY

Delivered from evil:
• 2 Corinthians 1:3-11; 12:1-10

QUESTIONS FOR THOUGHT AND DISCUSSION

• What is God doing now about evil? What will he do ultimately?
• What determines whether evil circumstances make or break us?
• Whom does God deliver from evil, and why?

The LORD has established his throne

in the heavens,

and his kingdom rules over all.

PSALM 103:19

CHAPTER 14

The Kingdom and the Power

As music can express the whole range of human feelings, so our Lord's pattern prayer covers the whole range of concerns with which life confronts the Christian disciple. Praise for our redemption (*Father*), adoration of God's transcendent greatness (*in heaven*), zeal for his glory (*hallowed be thy name*), longing for his triumph (*thy kingdom come*), and self-dedication to him (*thy will be done*) are all expressed in the first half; in terms of the common analysis of the elements of prayer as Adoration, Consecration, Thanksgiving, and Supplication (making the mnemonic A-C-T-S), all save the last are now covered. Then the supplications of the second half express our reliance on God for material needs (*give us . . . our daily bread*), our repentance over failures in faithfulness and our renouncing of mercilessness as a way of life (*forgive us*

. . . *as we also have forgiven*), and our sense of weakness in face of the forces of our spiritual foes (*lead us not into temptation, but deliver us*). Now, finally, following the traditional form of the prayer, we are led back to praise.

The doxology with which, following the older versions, we round off the Lord's Prayer is not in the best manuscripts. Nevertheless, it is in the best tradition! Doxologies (that is, acts of praise to God for his glory) pop up all through the Bible, and we saw before how in personal devotion praise and prayer grow out of, lead into, and stir up each other. Need felt and need met are their respective mainsprings, and praise for what God is, and does, is the strong support of hope in what he can, and will, do. So the more you praise, the more vigor you will have for prayer; and the more you pray, the more matter you will have for praise.

PRAYER AND PRAISE

Prayer and praise are like a bird's two wings: with both working, you soar; with one out of action, you are earthbound. But birds should not be earthbound, nor Christians praiseless. The clauses "who art in heaven" at the start and "as it is in heaven" in the middle are pauses for praise in the Lord's Prayer's flow, and if this closing doxology is not from Jesus' lips it certainly reflects his mind.

Prayer and praise are like a bird's two wings:
with both working, you soar; with one out of action,
you are earthbound. But birds should not be
earthbound, nor Christians praiseless.

Praise is linked to prayer here by the conjunction "for": "for thine is the kingdom and the power and the glory . . ." The connection of thought is that we ask our heavenly Father for provision, pardon, and protection with great confidence, since we know that for him to give this to his children on the one hand is within his *capacity*, and on the other is in line with the character he shows when he deals with men—that is, his *glory*. This, therefore, is an actual instance of praise for God's power and glory coming in to undergird prayer for the fruits of both.

KINGDOM AND POWER

Kingdom and power, as ascribed to God in this doxology, are two words expressing a single composite thought. (Grammarians call this idiom *hendiadys*: it is common in ancient literature.) The thought is of omnipotent control. *Kingdom* is used as in Psalm 103:19, "His kingdom rules over all": it denotes God's all-embracing mastery of the order of creation that is presupposed by the petition that God's kingdom in the other sense, the order of redemption touching everything, may "come." Satan, the prime example of how sin breeds cunning but saps intelligence and rots the mind, does not accept that the Lord is king in this basic sense and would dismiss this doxology—indeed, all doxologies—as false; but Christians know better, and praise God accordingly.

Power is the actual mastery that God's rule shows: not, then, naked arbitrary power, like that of a tornado, or a rogue elephant, or a dotty dictator, but unconquerable beneficence, triumphantly fulfilling purposes of mercy and loving-kindness "to us and to all men." It is the power by which God is good to all, and rescued Israel from Egypt, and raised Jesus Christ from the dead (Ephesians 1:19ff., etc.).

Psalms proclaiming God as the invincible gracious King (Psalms such as 47, 93, 97, 145, for a start) form the best exposition of "the kingdom and the power" in this doxology. Read them, ponder them, get them under your skin and into your heart—and join the Christian glee club! "It is good to sing praises to our God; for it is pleasant . . ." (Psalm 147:1).

FURTHER BIBLE STUDY

God on the throne:
- Daniel 4
- Psalm 145

QUESTIONS FOR THOUGHT AND DISCUSSION

- How do praise and prayer lead into and feed each other?
- What is "omnipotent control," and how is God exercising it in the world today?
- What is God's power like?

We all, with unveiled face, beholding the glory of the Lord, are being transformed into the same image from one degree of glory to another. For this comes from the Lord who is the Spirit.

2 CORINTHIANS 3:18

CHAPTER 15

And the Glory

In the New Testament, the word *glory* carries two inter-locked layers of meaning, each of which entails the other. Layer one is the manifested praiseworthiness of the Creator; layer two is the praise that this draws from his creatures. Which layer is "on top" depends on whether the reference is to the glory that God *has* and *shows* and *gives* or to that which he *is given*. For we in gratitude bless the God who in grace has blessed us, and this is to glorify the One who is even now glorifying us by remaking us in Christ's image (see 2 Corinthians 3:18; Ephesians 1:3; and compare Romans 1:21 with 8:17, 30). But that for which men give God glory is always something glorious, while the glories that God shows man are always intended to call forth praise.

GLORY SEEN

In the Old Testament, God displayed his glory in typical, visual form as an awe-inspiring expanse of bright light (the *shekinah*, as later Judaism called it). This was the sign of his beneficent presence in both the tabernacle and the temple (Exodus 40:34; 1 Kings 8:10ff.). The essential and abiding revelation of God's glory, however, was given by his great acts of merited judgment and unmerited love, and in his "name"—which was no mere label, as our names are, but a disclosure of God's nature and character. Jehovah (Yahweh, as modern scholars render it) means "I am (and will be) what I am (and will be)" (see Exodus 3:13-15), and the full statement of God's "name" declares precisely what he is and will be. This statement was made to Moses; when Moses asked God, "show me thy glory," God responded not only by a visual manifestation, but also by declaring, ". . . my name [is] 'the LORD' [Yahweh] . . . a God merciful and gracious, slow to anger, and abounding in steadfast love and faithfulness, keeping steadfast love for thousands, forgiving iniquity and transgression and sin, but who will by no means clear the guilty . . ." (Exodus 33:18–34:7). This moral character is the essential glory of God.

So, when the Word was made flesh in lowliness, having emptied himself of the glory he shared with the Father before creation, the breathtaking brilliance of the *shekinah* was hidden, save for the one isolated moment of transfiguration. Yet Jesus' disciples could testify, "we have beheld his glory," the glory of personal deity "full of grace and truth" (John 1:14; cf.

17:5; Philippians 2:7). Great as is the physical glory of *sheki-nah* light, the moral glory of God's redeeming love is greater. Those today whom God enlightens to understand the gospel never see the *shekinah*, but they behold the glory of God in the face of Jesus Christ (2 Corinthians 4:6).

GLORY GIVEN

When in the traditional Lord's Prayer doxology we ascribe the glory, along with the royal rule, to God forever, we are, first, telling God (and thus reminding ourselves) that he, our Maker and Redeemer, is, and always will be, glorious in all he does, especially in his acts of grace ("we give thanks to thee *for thy great glory*"); and, second, we are committing ourselves, now and always, to worship and adore him for it all ("*glory be to God on high*"). The doxology thus makes the Lord's Prayer end in praise, just as the Christian life itself will do: for while petition will cease with this life, the happy task of giving God glory will last for all eternity.

GLORY TO WHOM?

Now let us test our spiritual quality.

The principle of human sin (which is the devil's image in man) is this: glory is not God's, but mine. Accordingly, we parade what we think of as our glory, so that admiring watchers will give us glory. This is one facet of our pride: we call it vanity. Vain persons put on a show with their features, physical shape, clothes, skills, position, influence, homes, brains, acquaintanceships, or whatever they are most proud of, expect applause, and feel resentful and hurt if people do not play up to them and act impressed.

But Christians know that vanity is a lie, for it assumes that it is we who should be praised and admired for what we are; and that is not so. Christianity teaches us, not indeed to pretend that we lack qualities that we know very well that we have, but to acknowledge that all we have is God's gift to us, so that he should be praised and admired for it rather than we.

Christianity teaches us, not indeed to pretend that we lack qualities that we know very well that we have, but to acknowledge that all we have is God's gift to us, so that he should be praised and admired for it rather than we.

The test is to ask yourself how pleased, or how displeased, you become if God is praised while you are not, and equally if you are praised while God is not. The mature Christian is content not to have glory given to him, but it troubles him if men are not glorifying God. It pained the dying Puritan, Richard Baxter, the outstanding devotional writer of his day, when visitors praised him for his books. "I was but a pen in God's hand," he whispered, "and what praise is due to a pen?" That shows the mentality of the mature; they want to cry every moment, "Give glory to God—for it is his due, and his alone!"

What does this test tell us about ourselves?

FURTHER BIBLE STUDY

The way of doxology:
- Romans 11:33-36
- Ephesians 3:20ff.
- 1 Timothy 6:13-16
- Hebrews 13:20ff.
- Jude 24ff.
- Revelation 1:4-7

QUESTIONS FOR THOUGHT AND DISCUSSION

- What are the two meanings of the word *glory*, and what is the relationship between the two?
- What does God's character have to do with his glory?
- Is our ability to see God's glory limited by the absence of the *shekinah*? Why or why not?

For all the promises of God find their Yes in him. That is why it is through him that we utter our Amen to God for his glory.

2 CORINTHIANS 1:20

CHAPTER 16

Amen

When we say "Amen" after the Lord's Prayer, or any other prayer, what does it mean?

YES, THAT'S THE TRUTH!

Amen is a Hebrew word used in Old Testament and synagogue worship, whence it passed into Christian speech. In Scripture it not only ends prayer, showing an earnest wish to be heard, but also voices acceptance of such things as King David's orders (1 Kings 1:36) and God's threats (Numbers 5:22; Deuteronomy 27:17-26). Its root meaning is "true, firm, solid, certain," and what it expresses is an emphatic yes to what has been said: "definitely yes" as a man from the English Midlands might say, or "that's the truth" as in colloquial American. "So may it be," the usual paraphrase of "amen," is too weak: "amen" expresses not just a wish, but a committed confidence—"so *shall* it be."

"Amen" (best said loudly and with emphasis)
is our final profession of having meant what we have
said and identifying completely with the attitudes,
hopes, and goals that the prayer expresses.

"Amen" may either follow an utterance or precede it ("verily" in Jesus' formula, recurring more than fifty times; "verily I say . . ." is "amen" in the original). Either way, however, it underlines the utterance as an important one with which the speaker fully identifies. In 2 Corinthians 1:20, Paul speaks of Christians saying "amen" to God's promises, so glorifying him as true and trustworthy in what he says, "the God whose name is Amen" and whose "words are true" (Isaiah 65:16, NEB; 2 Samuel 7:28). Also, in 1 Corinthians 14:16 he envisages Christians saying "amen" to prayers of thanks uttered in public worship. The effect of saying "amen," assuming it is said with heart no less than voice, is to associate oneself with both promises and prayers in a way that makes them one's own.

YOUR PRAYER?

The traditional doxology teaches us to round off the Lord's Prayer with "amen." This is right. "Amen" (best said loudly and with emphasis) is our final profession of having meant what we have said and identifying completely with the attitudes, hopes, and goals that the prayer expresses. So the fittest way to end these brief studies in the prayer that takes a lifetime (and more) to master is with a checklist of the main items involved; and therefore I ask:

Do you identify with the trust in Jesus Christ as your own Savior, and the faith in God as your own God through him, and the recognition of every Christian as your own brother in God's family, that is expressed by "Our Father"?

Is the hallowing of God's name in and through you, whatever that may cost, your own controlling purpose in life? Do you want to see God triumph in his kingdom, and to see everything that does not match his perfection come to an end?

Will you labor and suffer for the kingdom, if need be, so as to become its agent, the means of bringing it into lives and situations where the gates have been locked against God?

Do you happily take God's will of command for your rule, and God's will of events for your destiny, knowing (by faith) that both are supremely good?

Is there any matter in which you are flying in the face of God's will of command, excusing yourself on the grounds of there being other commands that you faithfully keep? If so, what will you now do about it?

Do you see and know that unless God acts to provide for today's needs, and to pardon today's sins, and to protect you in today's temptations, you are lost?

Do you make it an issue of conscience never to bear a

grudge or cherish bitterness against anyone, but to show forgiving mercy always, because of the forgiving mercy that God always shows you?

Is there any person whom hitherto you have refused to forgive for what he or she did to you? Will you ask the Lord this moment to help you change your attitude, and get right with that person?

Do you make it your habit to watch and pray against temptation? Will you make it your habit from now on?

Is the Lord's Prayer really in your heart? Are you being honest when you say "amen" to it? "O God, make clean our hearts within us; and take not thy Holy Spirit from us." Lord, teach me how to pray, by teaching me how to live; for Jesus' sake; *amen*.

FURTHER BIBLE STUDY

The dangers of insincerity:
- Ecclesiastes 5:1-6
- Acts 5:1-11

QUESTIONS FOR THOUGHT AND DISCUSSION

- What does *amen* mean?
- Why is God called "the God whose name is Amen"?
- What is involved in saying "Amen" to the Lord's Prayer?